How to Start a Home Staging Business

ISBN-13: 978-1479248636

ISBN-10: 1479248630

Copyright Notice

All Rights Reserved © 2012 Monica Branna

HOW TO START A HOME STAGING BUSINESS

Monica Branna

I dedicate this book to everone– who has been lucky enough to have their lives touched by the joy, pleasure and sheer excitement of buying a new house...

Contents

Starting a Home Staging Business: An Overview

Have you been considering setting up a home staging business, but aren't quite sure if it's really the right venture for you?

Many people dream of starting their own business, but hesitate to do so because they have a family to take care of.

So they stay in corporate jobs, sitting at their desks all day, going through piles of documents. They don't necessarily enjoy the work, but they stay with it, thinking there's too much at risk for them to even try opening their own business. Are you one of these people willing to settle?

Do you want to start your very own home staging business?

Are you willing to do what it takes to turn your dream into reality or will you back down at the thought that a home staging business requires a lot of hard work and involves too much risk?

Can you imagine running a business that allows you to be creative and make use of your natural flair for home decorating?

If so, then you definitely should think about starting your own home staging business.

Also known as real estate enhancement, home staging is the act of decorating a house to make it attractive to potential buyers. Your job as a home stager is to help home owners, real estate agents, and home builders sell their properties more quickly and for the best price.

The good news is that there are literally thousands of houses that are being sold on any given day, which means there's a lot of business for a home stager. Home stagers are generally hired to emphasize a home's best features while downplaying or improving on its less attractive features.

Now, what's the difference between interior decorating and home staging?

Well, home staging is primarily about neutralizing the decor and removing the traces of a client's identity from the home such that it appeals to potential buyers with different preferences and tastes.

If you decide to start your own home staging business, you generally have two options:

1) Becoming a consultant and focusing on helping people stage their homes.

2) Doing the actual home staging yourself.

Creating interior designs, arranging decor, choosing colors, and laying out a home to look its best can indeed be great fun, and it can also be quite profitable too.

Running your very own home staging carries a lot of advantages. Among other things, you get to be your own boss, do things your way, set up your own schedule, and generally take control over your own future. A home staging also allows you to let your creative juices flow freely. The good news is that there have been many people who have successfully realised their dream of running their own home staging business and you, too, can realise that dream.

Pros and Cons of a Home Staging Business

A home staging business can indeed provide you with an excellent low-cost opportunity for earning good money and it can be the perfect home-based business for you to operate on either a part-time or full-time basis.

This means you may not have to leave your current employment even as you start your own business. If, at any time in the future, you feel that home staging is indeed the right career for you, then you can decide to concentrate on it full-time.

Of course, just like any other business venture, home staging comes with its own set of advantages and disadvantages. You'll have to be prepared to handle the disadvantages while enjoying the benefits of this business.

The Pros

There are several advantages to running your own home staging business, among which are the following:

1. A home staging business involves very low start-up costs as compared to other businesses. There's no need to carry inventory of any sort and the needed supplies are minimal. You also don't need to rent space for starters because you can easily run the business from a home office. Even advertising the business doesn't necessarily have to cost too much because the most effective way to get

clients for this business is through word-of-mouth advertising. Referrals from family, friends, realtors, and satisfied clients will definitely go a long way towards ensuring the success of your venture.

2. Regardless of whether the real estate market is currently strong or weak, the demand for home staging remains high. In fact, home staging is currently considered as one of the hottest growth businesses. As your own boss, you have full control of how fast you want your home staging business to grow. There are no external pressures.

3. There's no special licensing or training required, although getting certified can provide you with an added advantage, especially where building a reputation is concerned.

4. There's no need to recruit other people because this kind of business can be effectively run on your own. If you've done a bit of research into home-based businesses, then you're probably aware that there are lots of so-called business opportunities out there that require you

to purchase inventory and get others to join the business. Luckily, home staging isn't one of those businesses. It's a venture you can get into on your own without having to deal with recruiting pressures. This means you're not pressured into harassing family members and friends to invest in your "business opportunity."

5. There can be excellent financial rewards if you work hard at growing your home staging business. People may sometimes feel that home staging isn't really worth paying hundreds of dollars for, but once they realise that you can help them sell their property not only quickly, but also for a much better price than they'd otherwise get, they'll be more than willing to pay your asking price. Soon enough, you'll be earning the same amount for half a day's work as many people do in a week. Therefore, with just five clients in one week, you may earn more than you currently do in a month.

6. A home staging business doesn't require too much time of your time, which means you can still enjoy bonding moments with your family and see to other personal

demands even while doing hands-on work on your home staging business. You have full control of your schedule as you decide when to meet clients and can choose to work only during the day when your kids are in school. If you decide to start the business part-time, then you could probably meet with clients on evenings after work and do the actual work on weekends.

7. A home staging business allows you to enjoy variety and put your sense of adventure to good use. Projects in this business are typically short-term, lasting only for a few days or about two weeks at most. Each house you'll be staging is different, each client has different needs, and you'll likely get to visit neighbourhoods you didn't even know existed. This is the perfect opportunity to enter homes you previously only looked at from afar.

8. Because you're your own boss, you decide what particular projects you're going to take on and who you want to work with. And just in case you suddenly find yourself dealing with a particularly

difficult client, then you have the assurance that he won't be in your life for very long. Furthermore, if there are real estate agents that don't treat you with the kind of respect you deserve, then you can choose not to work with them again. After all, there are literally thousands of other agents you can choose to work with.

9. Since your projects are typically done in your clients' homes and meetings are usually conducted elsewhere, you won't have to worry if you own home's a mess; you can still run a successful home staging business. Besides your clients don't need to know where your office is and what it looks like. They're only concerned about what their own home will look like after you're done with it. After all, they're selling their house, not yours. What's important is that you present yourself well every time you meet with clients.

10. The demand for this business is currently growing as more and more homeowners learn about it from popular TV shows. Home staging is, in fact, considered a "hot" business these days. It allows you to

be creative with interior design and fashion trends. It also allows you to meet interesting people as you work on beautifying their homes.

If those reasons aren't enough for you, then consider the fact that you could earn about $35 to $75 or more per hour while enjoying all the benefits of being your own boss.

Furthermore, you don't need any special training or education to become a home stager. As long as you have natural talent and the commitment to succeed, then you can definitely break into this career.

The Cons

Of course as with any business a home staging business comes with its own set of disadvantages, the most significant of which are the following:

1. You may have a bit of difficulty finding the first clients who'll have enough faith in your advice and abilities to actually agree to pay for your services. This means it may take some time for you to build your portfolio and you may have to start

out by offering your services to friends and colleagues for free. If you decide to do this, make sure you do it for those who have a wide network of acquaintances and friends so they can refer you to others.

2. You may have to work several evenings and weekends, since your clients are probably free only during those times. Once you've built a solid reputation, though, you'll be able to take more control over your schedules.

Although there's no special degree or certification necessary to become a home stager, you can't just call yourself one and then expect to make it big in the home staging industry.

You'll need to familiarise the local real estate scene, learn how to price your services, identify potential clients, and build your portfolio, among other things. You'll also have to develop your people skills in order to achieve success in this business.

With a bit of self-education and short-term training, there's no reason why you can't build a successful home staging business.

Is Home Staging the Right Business for You?

The thought of having your very own home staging business can indeed seem like fun. Giving valuable advice on home design, rearranging furniture, de-cluttering homes, and transforming mediocre-looking houses into design masterpieces that sure to become bestsellers on the real estate market can definitely be a creative adventure anyone would enjoy.

But, do you really have what it takes to become a successful home stager?

Are you really tough enough for this kind of career?

You'll have to ask yourself some serious personal questions to find out if home staging is indeed the right business venture for you.

1. **Are you in excellent physical condition?**

   Remember that home staging involves a lot of pushing, pulling, lifting, and grunt work so it's definitely important to be in good shape.

If you aren't already regularly working out, then you'd better start before getting your home staging business up and running. After all, it may not be financially wise to keep paying someone else to do the grunt work for you.

2. Are you good at managing money?

During your first couple of years of in the home staging business, you'd do well to reinvest in your start-up company instead of taking hefty draws from the profits. Can you afford to do that? More importantly, will you be able to control your spending and maximise your profits? Financial management is crucial to the success of any business.

3. Are you good at design?

Take note that while there's no need for a degree in design to become successful in home staging, there may be a lot for you to learn in order to attain success. Having a natural eye for design is a huge advantage, of course, but it isn't enough to do well in this business.

There's a lot of difference between staging and decorating. Therefore, you have to make sure you have both the willingness and the capacity to learn what you need to in order to survive in the home staging industry.

4. Do you really believe in what you're doing?

A big part of attaining success has to do with believing in what you do. If you don't believe in staging, then how can you make others believe in you?

As long as you believe in what you do, you can easily open people's minds and change their lives as a home stager. And your excitement in the work itself can indeed become contagious.

5. Are you flexible?

Of course, we're not really talking about being able to be physically flexible. Being flexible with your time is important. The real estate business is a fast-paced industry and you'll probably be getting calls at any time for home staging projects.

You'll have to be willing and able to go with the flow. You should also be able to make quick decisions and act on projects just as quickly. People who need to sell their homes aren't likely to be willing to wait for you.

Where to Start?

Before you actually get your home staging business up and running, you have to acquire the necessary skills. You may want to enrol in short courses or participate in special training programs for this purpose. Self-education is also a good idea so try checking out interior design blogs and magazines and researching interior trends online.

It's also a good idea to get experience in home design through volunteer work or by getting jobs that help prepare you for a career in home staging.

And while it isn't a requirement, getting certified as a professional home stager may be a huge advantage for you when you finally start operating your business.

Naturally, you need to learn how to properly assess a home's current design such that you can recommend the best ways of staging it. You'll have to learn as much as you can about colours, textures, patterns, lines, and shapes.

You need to be able to come up with a good concept, organise and de-clutter the home, point out any cleaning or repairs that may be needed, and generally create a positive ambiance by setting the right temperature, proper lighting, pleasant smells, music, and other details.

Other than the basics on home staging, you'd also benefit from learning effective strategies for:

- Starting a home staging business with as little capital as possible.

- How to price your services and schedule your projects.

- How to identify potential clients.

- How to market your business effectively.

It's also a good idea to consider what other services you can possibly offer to complement your home staging business. (This can increase your profit margins too).

With talent, commitment, and the right attitude, you can surely make a success of your home staging business.

Start-Up Tips

Here are some tips to get you started:

- ✓ Read design magazines, watch home decorating shows, and visit home design stores. Ask specific questions about the styles commonly chosen in the stores to find out which is the most popular – modern, traditional, or contemporary.

  You should also ask about the most popular colours and if customers typically choose things according to color, scale, or texture. It would also help if you identified the market a particular magazine, show, or store is targeting.

  And when you look at furniture arrangements, try to think of other ways in which to arrange them and then decide if the one you're looking at is really the best arrangement for that room or space.

✓ As soon as you have business cards printed, you can start marketing your business and getting your first clients.

Hand your cards out to home owners with tips on how they can possibly sell their homes quicker and for a much better price. Also distribute your cards to realtors who may be able to pass a few referrals your way.

✓ You have the option of waiting until you have a steady stream of clients before you start buying props for the business, but you'll probably need a few framed pictures, books, magazines, lamps, fabrics, plants, area rugs, and place settings to start with.

Check if you have enough room in your basement, garage, or attic to store these items. If not, then you may consider getting in touch with a furniture rental company.

✓ Although a home staging business can easily be done on your own, it would really help for you to have at least one assistant (preferably male) who can move furniture for you, haul heavy items to and from your delivery van, and run errands when you're on a project. It may be a good idea to train an apprentice for this purpose.

✓ When you've gained enough experience, you might want to consider writing articles for local newspapers and trade magazines or giving talks or classes on home staging and decorating. This will go a long way towards promoting your business and widening your client base. It's also a good idea to create color brochures of your work, with before and after photos of homes you've staged. You can hand these brochures out each time you go to open houses.

✓ If you're going to establish a business website (and you should), then you have to make sure it ranks well on the results pages of the major search engines. Otherwise, people won't be able to find you and you won't be able to maximise the use of your site.

✓ When you set your rates, it's best to write down all of your expected costs and then divide the resulting amount with the total number of hours you intend to work. The result will be your base hourly rate. Of course, you'd want to add a little amount to cover labour costs. Always remember, though, that the primary purpose of home staging is for the homeowner to save – and even earn – money, so avoid making huge structural makeovers.

✓ Establish contacts with other businesses such as house painters, handyman services, and cleaning services. You can build mutually-beneficial relationships with these businesses. For example, you could tell your client that you can recommend a painter with very affordable rates if they want to have certain rooms in their home repainted. In the same way, the painter can refer you to some of their clients who may be thinking about selling their house.

✓ Local businesses are usually very well-connected. Therefore, you'd do well to use local businesses as much as you can. Buy furniture from local dealers, get your printing done by local printers, and rent storage facilities from local operators. These businesses may even turn out to be excellent sources of referrals for your home staging business.

✓ You may also want to consider offering a DIY service to homeowners who are on a tight budget. What you do in this case is take a tour of their home and then provide a list of suggested changes they can make in their home prior to putting it up for sale. You can choose to charge by the hour for this service or set a flat rate.

Pretty and profitable?

Aside from being enjoyable and providing you with an outlet for your creativity, a home staging business can also be very profitable. This is, in fact, among the biggest advantages of this business venture and many people have taken advantage of a home staging's potential for earning a great deal of money.

Of course, becoming successful isn't guaranteed in this business – or in any other business, for that matter. But, earning well while having fun is certainly something many people aspire to.

Identify your target market

Before you even open your home staging venture, you should already have decided what kinds of services you'll be selling and this decision will depend largely on your target market.

Identifying your target market is perhaps the very first thing you need to do because the kind of services you'll be selling is highly dependent on the type of individuals you'll be selling to.

Because women are the ones who are typically more interested in home and interior design, you may want to focus your home staging on their needs.

You should then do some research to find out what types of home design trends are currently popular with your identified group.

Remember that interior design is a very broad industry and your home staging needs to cover a specific niche in order to ensure success.

Once you've found your niche, you'll need to gain a deeper understanding of that niche and keep up with its trends so you can offer your customers only the best the world of design has to offer.

Treat them like kings

Customer service is another important component of running a home staging business. People love to receive special treatment and personalized service. Customers naturally love being treated like they're special and this is exactly what they get at a home staging. They're looking for personal service, professional and honest advice, and a wealth of information on the products and services they're interested in.

You may even know them by name if they're repeat customers. This part of the entire home staging experience is one you should never take for granted if you're serious about successfully running your own home staging venture.

You may start out as a one-man or woman operation, but sooner or later you're going to need help in running your home staging business, in which case you need to make sure you hire the right people.

Bear in mind that the home staging industry is constantly expanding and the number of home staging companies is growing. You can expect competition to be tough, which is why you need to take all the necessary steps to make your business stand out. Careful planning and close attention to detail should help you accomplish what you set out to do.

Once you have everything set up, you'll need to let your target market know of your existence so you can start building your initial customer base. You'd do well to develop an advertising and marketing plan that's sure to kick-off your operations.

Among your first steps should be making sure your opening day is a grand event. This is probably your best chance of drawing a lot of attention to your home staging business, so be sure to carry it out with a bang!

So now we have covered the overview let's get down to specifics.

Stay at home

You may also have heard some people saying that it's easy to start a staging business right from your own home. The hard truth is that it's not always easy to start any type of business from home.

This doesn't mean you should just forget about your dream of running your own staging, of course. It simply means you need to have the right expectations while your staging business is still in the planning stage.

If you seriously want to run your own staging business, then you'll need to develop close attention to detail, which is essential in this business.

You'll need to have adequate mathematical skills as well, so you can keep track of your business' accounting.

You also need to realise that there are important health and safety regulations a home staging business owner needs to adhere to.

In principle, starting a home staging business is quite simple, since it's easy enough to understand what needs to be done. But actually doing what needs to be done may not be as easy as you think.

Here are a few questions to consider:

- Do you have the necessary skills for market research?

- Can you put together a simple yet workable business plan?

- Do you have the kind of focus, patience, dedication, and passion necessary to execute your plan?

Start small

Perhaps you'd like to test the waters first by setting up a small home staging business that you can operate from home. This way, you get to start your dream business with minimal capital investment and gain the necessary experience that will help prepare you for the big leagues as well.

How to set prices

The first step in setting up the appropriate price structure is to determine how much each of your services cost to provide. This means you'll need to calculate the cost of every single thing you use, as well as the power and gas consumed in transporting goods. Once you've arrived at the cost of your service, you need to add your appropriate margin to determine your selling price.

Certificate Options

While certification certainly isn't required to get a home staging business started, it does provide you with a few advantages.

For one thing, potential clients may be likelier to trust a certified stager than one who builds his business on experience alone.

The good news is that there are plenty of available resources online that you can check if you decide to become a certified home stager. Getting certified is one of the best ways to give your business an image of legitimacy and assuring would-be clients of your reliability.

There are several avenues you can explore in the home staging business and these avenues may cause a bit of confusion at first. But, if you've already decided on the limits and scope of your home staging business, then it should be quite easy to choose the best certification option for your venture.

Here are the available certification options for a home staging business:

1. International

If there are no local home staging associations or companies in your area, then you should consider checking out the various training options offered by international staging organisations.

Most of these organisations offer their training online. Take note that they typically require you to pass two or more examinations when you apply for certification and the license you get will only certify you for that specific association.

This means you may still seek certification from other international organisations whenever you feel the need to.

2. State

Each state usually has its own local home staging authority and many of them offer training and affiliation opportunities you can take advantage of.

These opportunities will surely give you a much-needed advantage as you begin to establish your home staging business. Check with your local authority for listings.

3. Independent Organisations

When you do your homework you'll find that there are many independent staging organisations and companies that offer varying training courses and certifications. They can provide you with what you need to gain an edge in the home staging industry.

Take note that the certificate you get will likely only reflect the name of the organisation or company awarding it. Despite this, and independent certificate can still help you build a solid reputation and you may proudly display it on your wall for potential clients to see.

Professional certifications of any kind will definitely add to your credibility in the eyes of would-be clients.

Remember that certifications are actually nothing more than formalities that show your clients you have a seal of approval from industry authorities. That being said, you shouldn't get too hung up on getting certified as a home stager.

Rather, you should place more focus on the actual process of working for that certification because that's where you get some valuable learning that can help you in your business.

Among other things, the application process requires you to go through a brief training course, which provides you with the opportunity to learn about the tricks of the trade and build your portfolio.

Bear in mind that the success of your home staging business lies not on your certificates, but on your ability to build your network and the efficiency and professionalism of your work.

Naming Your
Home Staging Business

Choosing a company name can be the most fun part of starting a company. It can also be one of the most important.

After all, having the right home staging business name can be a very effective advertising tool. Among other things, it can give prospective customers a general idea of what your company does and what you have to offer.

In the same way, choosing the wrong name is likely to drive would-be customers away.

Here are a couple of things to remember when choosing a home staging business name:

Keep it short and memorable

Needless to say, a short company name is much easier to remember than a lengthy one.

Choosing a short name doesn't just involve using less words, but also words with less syllables.

But, aside from being short, your home staging business name also has to be catchy so as to promote better name recall.

You are your name

This means your company name should reflect the company's personality.

It should give people a general idea of what services you provide or what benefits they can get from patronizing your home staging business.

You need to have an image which you want your home staging business to project and the name you choose must fit that image.

More importantly, you have to choose a name your target customers can easily connect with. Now, you know the basics of choosing a company name and you realize how important a name is to your business.

However, you shouldn't take the process of choosing a name too seriously.

While the company name does have to reflect its personality, it doesn't really have to define your company completely.

Take note that venturing into other related businesses is a normal part of any company's growth, so there is a real possibility that you may have to change your home staging business name from time to time.

Again, the name of your home staging business is important, but you shouldn't get hung up on the process of choosing it.

As long as you make sure that it's memorable, it tells people what your home staging business is about, and you're proud of it, then you're good to go.

Drawing Up a Business Plan

Developing a new home staging business naturally requires a good foundation, and building such a foundation begins with having a sound business plan.

Remember that the business plan is an essential part of documenting a start-up business' financial goals, business objectives, and marketing plans.

Implementation of all your home staging business ideas can only successfully begin once you've completed your business plan.

Choosing the Right Format

You probably already know that a business plan ranks among the most vital components of starting your home staging business and ensuring its success.

But, how exactly do you make a good business plan?

Well, there are several variations and templates you can choose from.

What's important is for you to choose the one that's best suited to the kind of enterprise you'll be running and to the purpose for which you're making the plan in the first place.

Here are some of the things you need to take into consideration:

1. Your Target Audience

There are two types of business plan.

a. There are business plans intended for an internal audience and these plans are usually part of your home staging business growth strategy; they're also usually referred to as strategic plans.

b. There are also plans meant for external audiences and the purpose of these plans is usually to attract financing, suppliers, or talent for your home staging business.

If the purpose of your business plan is primarily to get funding, then the document will typically be in condensed form, or a sort of summary of a more comprehensive business plan.

Such a version is generally known as a *funding proposal* or a *business opportunity document* and it's usually followed by the larger plan.

A business plan can indeed be a very useful document, so it's important to clearly define the audience for which it is intended.

2. What Goes Into the Plan?

Remember that a business plan needs to be comprehensive and that it's essentially created to put into writing what you envision for your home staging business venture.

Your home staging business plan should contain:

- An executive summary,
- The background and history of your company,
- A clear description of your home staging business concept,
- Your marketing analysis and development plan,
- Your operations and production assessment,
- Your financial assessments and projections,
- Your human resources management assessment and plan,
- Your business implementation plan,
- An identification of resources,

- The proposed investor deal structures wherever appropriate,
- A survival strategy that describes potential risks and mitigation measures,
- Your home staging business growth strategy,
- Your exit strategy,
- Appendices.

If that seems daunting, don't worry.

Some of the components of your business plan may be longer than others and some of them are optional, depending on your target audience, the format you choose to adopt, and the purpose of your plan.

What's important is for your intended reader to clearly grasp the value proposition, understand why your home staging business is expected to succeed, and how that success will be achieved.

If you're pitching the plan to potential investors, (or most probably the bank) then they should quickly understand your proposed deal structure and the possible returns.

3. What Length To Make Your Plan

The average business plan typically consists of 20 pages, though there are some that contain a hundred pages or more. The length of your plan will depend largely on its purpose and your target audience.

If the primary purpose of your business plan is to attract investors, then you can expect it to contain more details and therefore be lengthier than a plan that's primarily for communicating your home staging business growth strategy.

In the same way, the business plan for a venture with a relatively simple concept should be a lot more concise than one that's made for a highly complicated enterprise.

4. Should You Use a Template or Pay a Consultant?

Many people are also confused as to whether they should hire a consultant to help them write their business plan or simply use a template for guidance.

Well, it can be quite tempting to use a template or get someone else to make the plan for you.

However, it's still best if you write the plan yourself even if you do decide to get some guidance from a consultant. After all, who knows your business better than you?

A solid business plan is perhaps the easiest way for you to communicate your home staging business ideas to your target audience as well as to help you prevent problems and identify business growth strategies.

It can also be your most valuable tool when you're in search of funding for your home staging business.

Remember, though, that instead of treating it as a blueprint or a strict manual which you should implement to the letter, the plan should be seen as more of a guide in operating your home staging business.

TIP: Even if you don't have an immediate audience for your plan, the document and even the process itself will definitely prove to be of value to your business in the long run.

Preparing a solid business plan for all the right reasons can indeed increase your chances of attaining success in your home staging business.

How to Write the Executive Summary

The executive summary generally serves as the introduction to your formal and comprehensive business plan.

You could even say that this is Part 1 of your business plan.

It contains a summary of your home staging business proposition, present business status, financial projections, and the key elements for success.

Although it's often tempting to just rush through this component of your business plan, always remember that an executive summary is likely to be the very first thing your target investors or banking officeals will read in the document.

It basically tells the reader the status of the company currently, and where it's expected to go. Many people aren't likely to read the remainder of the plan if the executive summary doesn't catch their interest, so it's really very important to do this right.

The importance of the executive summary lies in the fact that it tells your reader exactly why you believe your home staging business will be a success.

Brevity is the key to a solid executive summary, which generally ranges from half a page to a maximum of two pages. Writing anything longer puts you at risk of losing the reader's attention and appearing unfocused. If you can keep the summary under one page without sacrificing quality, then do so.

Note: Although it serves as the introduction, it's best to write the executive summary after you've completed your business plan. After all, it is basically a shorter version of your plan.

To keep the summary consistent with the plan itself, it should have the following components:

1. Your Mission Statement

Your business plan's executive summary is be the best place for you to express your mission statement. Make sure that statement is concise and explains in as few words as possible the existence of your home staging business, its goals, and how you plan to achieve those goals.

In short, it should explain your home staging business thrust to the reader. Remember to keep your mission statement focused and direct, leaving no room for confusion as regards what your home staging business venture is all about.

2. What's Your Business Concept?

In describing your home staging business concept, you'll need to offer some details about the kind of home staging business you'll be running, who your target customers are, and what your competitive advantages are.
You may point out that you're filling a void you've identified in the market, offering better prices for comparable services in the industry, or offering a better service than what's currently available.

3. A Little Background

You may also want to give your reader an idea of when your venture began, who the founders are and what functions they perform, how many employees you have (or plan to hire), and where the home staging business is located and if there are any subsidiaries or branches. A description of your offices and facilities as well as the services your offer would also be a good idea.

4. Your Home Staging Business Status and Financial Outlook

You'll also need to give a short description of the current status of your home staging business.

Explain if your business is still in the conceptualization stage, if you've already started setting it up, or if it's already fully operational and you're simply planning to expand.

You should also mention your expected costs and your financial projections for both the short term and the long term.

This will give potential investors an idea of how much capital you need and if your business venture matches the kind of opportunity they're currently looking for.

If you already have existing investors, then you'd do well to provide some information on them as well.

5. Key Factors for Success

The reader of your business plan will also appreciate getting a preview of the key factors for home staging business success.

These factors depend on your situation, of course, but it generally includes technology patents, strategic partnerships, market factors and economic trends.

If your home staging business is already fully operational and you've had some successful projects worth noting (you may have been the first to offer a certain service in the industry), then you should include that as well.

Finally...

All in all, your business plan's executive summary should provide its reader with a quick but insightful glimpse into the plan itself.

It's advisable to highlight everything except the mission statement in bulleted lists. Include all of the important points without revealing too much, since each section is discussed in detail within the plan itself, anyway.

More importantly, make sure the summary sells the proposal on its own as much as possible, just in case reader doesn't read your plan. It does happen!

Note: It's also a good idea to draw up a table of contents right after the executive summary so the reader will know where he can find each section in the plan itself.

If you're still in the process of setting up your home staging business, then you likely won't have much to write as regards to some of the areas listed above. In that case, focus on your own experience and expertise in the field, and the circumstances that led to your home staging business concept.

Tell your target readers how you plan to set your home staging business apart from the competition and convince them that there's indeed a need for your business within your target niche or industry.

Company History

After the executive summary, your business plan should contain a section covering your business background or company history.

The length of this portion and how it's told will depend largely on how far along your home staging business is in terms of operations and development.

Naturally, the business history of a venture that's just starting is totally different from one that's been operating for some time.

It should be about one page long, though it's understandable for a start-up company's history to cover less than an entire page.

What to Include

In this section, you should be able to illustrate how the various elements of your home staging business venture fit together and form one successful enterprise.

You should also include some background information on the nature of the home staging business itself and identify the factors that are expected to facilitate its success.

Furthermore, don't forget to mention the specific market needs you're planning to satisfy and the ways and methods in which you expect to satisfy these needs.

If possible, you should also identify the specific individuals or groups of people whom you believe have those needs.

An example of a specific market could be:

Couples aged 30 to 50 with an income of $200,000 within 50 miles of your location.

How It All Started

Among the things you should include in the company history portion of your business plan is the origin of your home staging business concept.

This explains how you first came upon the idea for your home staging business and why you decided to pursue that idea. You should also indicate the progress you've made so far as regards operating and growing your business venture. If you're still in the process of starting your business, then say so.

NOTE: It's also a good idea to mention the problems you've encountered along the way and how you handled each of them.

Potential investors and business partners will surely appreciate knowing that they're dealing with someone who's not afraid to deal with challenges from time to time.

Projected Short-Term Growth

You would also do well to include your short-term business growth plans in this section, so the reader will know that you've thought about your venture carefully and that you have concrete plans for its growth.

NOTE: If you're just starting a new home staging business, then you may want to include a bit of personal history along with your background.

Among the things you can include are your educational history, technical skills, areas of expertise, relevant professional club memberships, and other home staging businesses you may have started or companies you worked for.

TIP: You may even want to share your areas of inexperience or weaknesses and how you intend to compensate for these areas.

Your target investors would definitely appreciate knowing that you're aware of the things you need to improve on and are making concrete efforts at improving them.

Finally…

In summary, the company history section of
your business plan should provide an interested
reader with a much better idea of how your
home staging business came to be and who you
are as a businessperson. Again, the key is to
keep this section concise and avoiding unwanted
information.

Organization and Management

This section of your plan includes the following:

- Your company's organizational structure

- The profiles of your management team

- Details about company ownership

- The board of director's qualifications

It's important for you to answer the question of
who does what when you prepare this section.

Explain what each person's background and
qualifications are. Tell your reader exactly why
you've brought or are bringing these people into
your organization and management team.

What exactly are they responsible and accountable for?

NOTE: You may think this section of the plan is unnecessary if you're setting up a small venture with less than five people on your team, but anybody reading your business plan needs to know who's in charge. Therefore, you should still provide a description of every department or division, along with their functions, regardless of the size of your company.

If there's an advisory board for your business, then you should also identify who's on it and how you plan to keep each member on the board.

- What salary and benefits do you plan to provide for members of your team?

- Will you be offering incentives? If so, what are they?

- How do you plan to handle promotions?

In this section of your business plan, you need to reassure your audience that the people on your team aren't going to be just names on your company letterhead.

What's Your Structure?

One very simple yet effective way of presenting your organizational structure is by creating an organizational chart and then providing a narrative description of the chart.

By doing this, you don't leave anything to chance, you're making sure the functions and responsibilities of each team member has been carefully thought out, and you've ensured that someone's in charge of each and every function in your home staging business.

Therefore, no function is taken for granted and there'll be no overlapping of responsibilities.

TIP: Remember that this kind of assurance is very important to your reader, especially if that reader is a potential investor.

Management Profiles

Ask any business expert and he'll probably tell you that among the most significant success factors in any business is the track record and ability of the management team.

This is why it's important for you to provide your reader with a background of the key members of the management team. (Don't worry if your just starting out. You won't have management staff at this stage).

Specifically, you'd do well to provide resumes that indicate the name, position and the corresponding functions, primary responsibilities and level of authority, educational background, skills and experience, number of years on your team (unless it's a start-up company), compensation level and basis, previous employment and track record, industry recognitions received, and community involvement.

TIP: When you indicate the track record of your team, be sure to quantify their achievements.

For example, instead of saying:

"Extensive experience in managing a sales department"

you could say:

"Successfully managed a sales department of ten people for 15 years."

It's also a good idea to highlight how the key members of the management team complement your own experience and expertise.

If you're starting a new home staging business, then show your reader how the unique experiences of each member of your team can contribute to your business venture's overall success.

Company Ownership

Aside from the organizational structure, this section of the plan should also describe the legal structure and provide important ownership information regarding your home staging business.

- Has the business been incorporated? If so, then is it an S or a C corporation?

- Is your business a partnership?

- If so, then is it a limited or general partnership?

- Or are you the sole proprietor of your home staging business?

The most important pieces of information you should include in this section are the owner/s' names, ownership percentage, form of ownership, degree of involvement of each owner within the business, common stock, and outstanding equity equivalents.

Board Qualifications

Take note that there's a huge advantage to setting up an unpaid board of advisors for your company, as it can provide you with the kind of expertise the company is otherwise unable to afford.

Simply by enlisting the help of some successful businessmen who are popular in the industry and including them in your advisory board, you'll definitely go far in enhancing the credibility of your company and encouraging a perception of expertise.

If the company has a board of directors, then you need to provide the names of the board members, their respective positions in the BOD, their background, the extent of their involvement with the home staging business, and their expected contribution to its success.

Market Analysis

You may be a hundred percent confident about the quality of the service your home staging business has to offer, but unless you're able to connect with your target customers, quality won't do you much good.

You'll have to get your service into your customers' hands, so to speak, to get the necessary sales.

And that's why you need market analysis. This section of your business plan should be used to illustrate your knowledge of the industry. You may also use it to present highlights and conclusions from the marketing research data you've collected.

For your analysis to be reliable, you need to study the three Cs of marketing:

1. Company

2. Customer

3. Competition

Of course, it's understandable that you should be aware of your company's strengths and weaknesses, but you should also know the same things about your competitors so you'll get a better idea of how to deal with them.

More importantly, you need to know who your customers are and what their needs and wants really are.

When you prepare the company analysis component of this section, you'll need to describe the primary industry to which your business belongs, the industry's current size and historic growth rate, the industry's characteristics and trends, and the industry's major customer groups.

All these will put into perspective the description you'll provide of the company you've established or are planning to establish.

Who Are Your Target Customers?

In choosing and defining your target customers, make sure that you narrow it down to a size that you're sure you can manage.

Many business owners make the mistake of trying to provide everything to everybody at once. Slow and sure is often a better philosophy where your business is concerned.

This section of your plan should include information that identifies the unique characteristics of your target customers including:

- Their needs

- The extent to which these needs are being met

- Demographics.

It's also a good idea to identify your target market's geographic location, who among them makes the major decisions, and any market trends that may affect your business.

The size of your target market should also be indicated in this section, along with your expected market share gains and the reason for these expected gains.

You should also indicate your pricing schedule as well as your gross margin targets and whatever discount structures you may be planning.

You'd also do well to identify what resources you plan to use to get information as regards your target market, the media you'll be using to reach the market, your target market's purchasing cycle, and the socio-economic trends likely to affect your target market.

If all this sounds complicated don't worry, just break down each section and do it one at a time.

Your Competition

Of all the Cs you need to study, your competition may be the toughest, especially if you're new to the industry.

The first thing you need to do is study your direct competitors.

If you're planning to operate a home staging business in your district, then you're likely to get direct competition from the likes of the larger multi-national home staging businesses.

So it pays to examine all the possible options on how you can set your home staging business apart.

It's important for you to identify your direct competitors according to product or service line and market segment.

You should then assess their weaknesses and strengths, determine the level of importance of your own target market to your competitors, and identify the barriers that may pose a challenge as you enter your target niche.

This may include high investment costs, changing technology, existing patents or trademarks, customer resistance, and a difficulty in finding quality personnel.

You'd also do well to determine the market share of each key competitor and then provide an estimate of the time it'll take for new competitors to enter the niche.

Aside from looking for ways to set yourself apart from the competition, you'll also want to see how your business fits into the marketplace itself.

In doing so, you'll have to consider the strengths and weaknesses of your competitors, the possibility of competitors leaving the marketplace and new ones entering it, the services your competitors are relying on for a majority of their revenue, and effective ways of overcoming possible threats from substitute services.

Developing Your Marketing Strategy

Once all three Cs have been addressed, you should be ready to start developing your marketing program.

This basically involves an analysis of what's known as the "four Ps."

They are:

1. Product,

2. Place,

3. Price,

4. Promotion.

Product, of course, refers to what you plan to sell (in this case your home staging service)

Place refers to where you plan to sell it (office, online, or both).

Price refers to the amount you'll charge for each service you'll be offering.

And Promotion refers to the incentives and other promotional strategies you plan to use in order to get your target market to try your services.

To put it simply, a marketing strategy is your way of drawing in customers, which is indeed very important since customers are essentially the lifeblood of any business venture.

There isn't a single way of approaching a marketing strategy. What's important is for your strategy to be uniquely applicable to your home staging business and part of a continuing evaluation process that aims to facilitate business growth and success.

In conducting a "four Ps" analysis, you'll likely conduct some market tests and you'd do well to include the results of these tests in this section of your business plan. All other details of the tests may be attached as an appendix.

The information you provide in this section may include the number of customers who participated in the tests, demonstrations or any information provided to the participating customers, the degree of importance of satisfying the needs of your target market, and the percentage of participants who expressed desire to take advantage of your products and/or services.

After creating your marketing strategy, you'll also need to draw up a sales strategy, which outlines the methods you'll be using to actually sell the services you plan to offer.

There are two very important elements of a good sales strategy.

- The first is your sales force strategy, which determines if you'll be employing internal sales personnel or independent representatives.

You should also identify the number of people you plan to recruit for your company's sales force as well as the recruitment and training strategies you'll be using.

You'd also do well to present the compensation packages you've lined up for your sales personnel.

- The second element of a sales strategy is a description of the sales activities you've lined up for the company.

A sales strategy is made more manageable when broken down into activities.

For example, you could start with identifying prospective customers and then prioritizing your prospects according to those who have the highest potential of buying your products.

From this outline of activities, you can easily determine the number of prospects you may have to get to make a sale and the average amount you'll likely earn from each sale.

You'll also need to draw up a solid market development plan in order to make your market analysis work to your advantage.

While the information in your development plan is likely to come into play only when your company has been established and operational for at least a few years, potential investors will surely appreciate the fact that you've already envisioned your company's growth and evolution.

Among other things, your development plan should provide answers to the following questions:

➢ Is the market for the services you offer currently growing?

➢ Are you planning to offer line extensions or new services within your first few years of operations?

➢ Does the market development plan you've crafted offer ways of increasing the overall demand for your services within the industry?

➢ Are there alternative ways of making your company more competitive?

Remember that the market analysis is a vital part of your business plan and it's likely to take up a large part of the plan itself.

This is why it's necessary to conduct a thorough research on the competition and on the market you're planning to enter.

Finally...

You may have the best service in the market, but without an organized and well-crafted market analysis and development plan, you still won't be able to guarantee success.

You market analysis helps you identify a clear roadmap of how to bring your services to your target customers.

Financial Projections

Making financial projections for a start-up home staging business can be described as both science and art.

Investors may want to see you spell out financial forecasts in cold, hard numbers, but it's not really that easy to predict the financial performance of your home staging business several years from now, especially if you're still in the process of raising capital.

Simply put, this is the part where you formally request funding from potential investors and you do that by illustrating how much funding you need for start-up as well as within the first five years of operations.

If you already have an existing business and are looking towards expansion, then you may reflect the funding requirements for the expansion itself.

Potential investors are also sure to appreciate some historical data as regards the financial performance of your company, particularly within the last three years or so, depending on how long you've been in business. If you have any collateral that can possibly be used to secure a loan, then that's worth noting as well.

Difficulty aside, financial projections are requirements for a solid business plan and you'll really have to deal with them if you truly want to catch your prospective investors' attention.

Regardless of whether your business is a start-up or a growing venture, you'll still need to provide historical and/or projected financial data.

Here are a few useful tips:

1. **Don't let spreadsheets intimidate you**

All financial projections necessarily start with spreadsheet software, with Microsoft Excel being the most commonly used; chances are great you already have the software on your computer.

Other than this, there are also some special software packages that can help you with financial projections. These packages often provide flexibility, which allows you to weigh alternate scenarios or change assumptions quickly whenever necessary.

2. **Create short-term projections as well as medium-term projections**

Specifically, your prospective investors should see financial projections for the first year of operations, broken down into monthly projections.

You should also provide a three-year financial projection that's broken down into yearly projections and a five-year financial projection.

TIP: It's advisable, however, to keep your five-year projection separate from your business plan, but readily available in case a potential investor asks to see it. When you project business growth, be sure to consider the current state of your market, trends in labour and costs, and the possibility of needing additional funding for future expansion.

3. Make sure start-up fees are accounted for

Never forget to include fees for permits, licenses, and equipment in your short-term projections. You should also keep the difference between variable and fixed costs in mind when making your projections and differentiate between the two wherever necessary. Variable costs are usually placed under the "costs for goods sold" category.

4. Go beyond your income statement

While your income statement is the basic measuring tool by which projected expenses and revenue can be conveyed, a solid financial projection will go beyond that to include projected balance sheets that show a breakdown of your assets, liabilities, and equity, among other things.

You'd also do well to include cash flow projections that reveal cash movement through the company within a given period. Estimates of the amount you plan on borrowing as well as expected interest payments on those loans should also be included.

Furthermore, you should make sure your financial projections are all in accordance to the GAAP.

TIP: If you're new to financial reporting or don't understand the last paragraph, then you may want to consider hiring an accountant to review your projections.

5. **Offer two scenarios only**

Although you need to go beyond the simple income statement, remember that where financial projections are concerned, potential investors really want to see only two scenarios:

The best- and worst-case scenarios. Anything more than those two are superfluous and may just cause unnecessary confusion, so skip it.

Finally...

To sum up, this section should tell potential investors how much money you need now and in the near future, your preferred type of funding and terms, and how you intend to use the funds.

NOTE: Take note that the intended use of the funds is a vital piece of information for potential investors and would-be creditors, which is why you need to explain it in this section.

It's also important to include all pertinent business-related information that can possibly affect the future financial situation of your company.

A trend analysis for your financial statements is also very helpful, especially if you present it with graphs, as this is easier to see.

TIP: Above all, you should strive to make reasonable and clear assumptions.

As previously mentioned, financial forecasting is both a science and an art. You'll need to make several assumptions, but you'll also have to be realistic when making those assumptions. Going overboard will likely raise red flags for potential investors, so always make sure your projections are backed up by solid research.

Calculating Your Start-up Costs

What are start-up costs?

These are the expenses you have to deal with before your new home staging business can actually begin operations and earn revenue.

The concept of start-up costs is very important in tax law because these costs are not considered as deductible expenses, unlike most of the other business costs. You will, instead, need to amortize these costs over the course of a few months or years.

This means you'll only be able to deduct part of the start-up costs each year.

And you can only determine and take full deduction on your other expenses after you have determined start-up costs.

The first step

The first step in calculating the start-up costs of your business is to gather all of the expense receipts from business-related transactions.

Next, determine the exact date when your home staging business opened and then separate the receipts into two piles: one pile for the expenses from before your business opened and another pile for expenses incurred after the opening day.

You see the reason why many people say it's so much easier to start a home-based staging business than opening one at a retail location is that it requires significantly fewer equipment and materials.

Consequently, a home-based business would entail much less start-up capital as well. In fact, starting a home staging business can be the perfect test run that can help you determine if it is indeed a wise decision to push through with a full-scale commercial staging operation.

Once you've decided on the location of your staging, you can start drawing up the budget for your start-up costs.

Starting a home staging business with what you already have on hand is advisable not only because it's cost-effective, but also because it lets you work with equipment and materials you're already familiar with.

You could simply add more equipment and materials as your business grows and the need for equipment arises.

The next step is to remove all of the receipts for items such as research costs, taxes, and deductible interest from the pile receipts before opening day.

These costs can immediately be deducted. Finally, add together all the remaining receipts belonging to your "before opening date" pile. The sum is your total start-up costs, which have to be amortized.

Amortization is usually set over a period of 18 months, and expenses like hiring and training costs, pre-opening advertising, and travel expenses to meet potential suppliers are usually included in the amortized start-up costs.

How to Obtain
Small Business Grants

When starting a business there can be some huge barriers standing in your way, among the biggest of which are start-up costs and other business-related expenses.

You may be planning to take out a loan for the purpose of starting your home staging business. Why don't you consider applying for grants from the government or from private organizations instead?

There are several reasons why grants are better than a loan, the most obvious of which is the fact that grants don't need to be repaid.

How exactly can you obtain a business grant and turn your simple idea into a thriving home staging business?

Read on to find out. The Catalog of Federal Domestic Assistance is a good place for you to search for a specific grant you can apply for because it contains a list of all grants available for small home staging businesses.

The catalog also indicates what type of business qualifies for a particular grant, so you can immediately determine which grants your home staging business is likely to qualify for.

Another option is for you to visit the Small Business Administration's website, which promotes federal grant programs that offer almost $2 billion to small businesses, particularly those focusing on providing technological solutions to existing business issues.

Once you have identified the grant programs you will be applying for, you should start preparing a business plan.

Take note that grant organizations base their approval or rejection of your application on the contents of your home staging business plan.

- Your plan should therefore include a statement of purpose that is clearly written and effectively defines the goals of your company.

- A good home staging business description, an outline of your short-term and long-term goals, a discussion on planned marketing strategies, and a projected financial analysis should also be part of your plan.

The financial section of your plan is very important because organizations usually measure the worth of a candidate based on how you plan to use the grant money.

You should therefore make sure that your financial analysis and hypothetical budget are both conservative and realistic.

When your home staging business plan is complete, it's time to create your actual grant proposal.

If you have previous experience in creating such a proposal, then you can save some money by writing the proposal yourself.

However, if you've never written a grant proposal before, then it would be wise to hire the services of a professional writer.

Make sure your proposal includes schematics, reports, and some basic information on planned projects that are likely to be influenced by the grant funds.

Furthermore, grant reviewers are likely to appreciate such attention to detail, which may be seen as a strong commitment to your product.

In this case, the reviewers will be more likely to approve your applying for grant funds. Complete your grant application by including an updated list of contacts.

This list should start with the contact details of the top-level employees.

It should also include the contact details of individuals who can provide important details on the supplementary materials included in your application.

Make sure that all pertinent information on your home staging business and requested files by the grant organization are included in your application.

If your application lacks any of these files, then the grant is likely to be denied or the processing could be very slow. Submit your application only when you're sure that it's complete.

It's also a good idea to have your grant application reviewed by family, friends, and colleagues so grammatical errors can be cleared up and anything you may have overlooked can be pointed out to you.

And as a final review process, you should schedule a reading session together with your staff, so you can correct any identified problems. Above all, you should be patient.

Take note that the process of getting approved for grants may take longer to complete than the process of getting approved for loans.

This is because grant applications are reviewed a number of times and most grant organizations have to go through thousands of applications at a time.

Getting Insurance for Your Home Staging Business

So, you have an idea for a good home staging business venture; you even have the name for your new home staging business already.

And you've also proceeded to create a business plan and a proposal for a grant application. The next step is to get adequate insurance.

This is actually one of the most important steps you need to take when starting a home staging business.

The good news is that there are lots of great places where you can get good advice on the different types of insurance that you may need for your new home staging business.

An insurance agent is probably the best person for you to approach if you're looking for advice on getting insurance for your home staging business.

More specifically, you should hire the services of an agent for an insurance company that specializes on home staging business insurance rather than a general insurance company.

You have to understand that you'll be dealing with a totally different set of risks and challenges with a business than you would with a car or with your home.

Getting insurance from a company that specializes in home staging business insurance assures you that the agent you're dealing with really knows what he's talking about.

You can expect the insurance agent to lay out several different insurance options for you. These options can range from liability insurance for your home staging business to auto insurance.

You may also be offered property insurance as well as loss of business coverage, which protects your interests in case a fire breaks out and you end up without a business to run for a month or so.

It's important for you to ask questions and make sure you understand what each type of insurance covers you for so you can be sure to make an informed decision as to which types of insurance you're going to get.

More often than not, you'll be presented with more insurance options than you can afford. There's also a possibility that the insurance agent you're consulting will present you with more insurance options than your business actually needs.

This makes it even more important for you to understand what each type of insurance covers. Furthermore, the start of a business is usually a time when you will have to take a few risks by taking out less insurance than your home staging business needs.

You'll have to decide how much you can afford to spend for insurance and which type of insurance is the most needed by your home staging business.

Once you've determined this, you can leave the other types of insurance for later.

Most home staging businesses start only with loss of business coverage, others with liability insurance.

The point is to get only the most important insurance coverage that you can afford for starters.

As your company grows, it will become more important for you to protect your home staging business' assets.

And the good news is that you may able to afford it at that time.

Aside from the insurance that you have previously identified as a need for your home staging business, there may also be other types of insurance that your customers expect you to have.

You can work on getting these additional insurance types when the right time comes.

How to Trademark Your Home Staging Business Name and Logo

If you have just put up a new home staging business, you should be careful not to stop at choosing a name and logo for it.

You should also make sure that the name and logo you chose is adequately protected.

This is especially important if one of your business goals is to create an instantly recognizable brand.

The best way to protect your business name and logo is to have it trademarked.

Take note that a trademark is also used to protect symbols, drawings, and any other character associated with your home staging business, much like a patent protects inventions.

The whole process of getting your business name and logo trademarked is a relatively simple one.

However, it often takes several months for your trademark registration to really become official.

Following is a quick guide on how you can protect your business name and logo by getting it trademarked.

1. Choose the name and design the logo for your new home staging business.

    You have to make sure, of course, that the name and logo you choose are not yet being used by any other company. More importantly, you need to ensure that such name and logo have not already been trademarked by someone else. You can check the database of the official trademark office to make sure you won't run into any legal problems with your chosen name and logo.

2. Once you have established that your chosen home staging business name and logo are not yet trademarked, request for and fill-out the necessary paperwork. Once the paperwork has been filled out and submitted to the Patent and Trademark Office, the processing of your application for registration will officially begin.

3. Allow five months for the processing to be completed.

If five months have passed and you still have not received any notification of your trademark having been filed, you may check on its status. Take note, though, that it usually takes between five and seven months for a trademark registration process to be completed.

4. Once you receive notification of your trademark having been filed, obtain a copy of it from the trademark office. Take note that you will be asked for your registration number when you make the request for a copy of your trademark certificate.

5. Between the fifth and sixth year of your trademark registration, make sure that an "Affidavit of Use" is filed, so as to prevent other companies from using your trademarked name and logo. You should remember to file two other affidavits as well before every 10-year period of owning the trademark has passed.

Writing an LLC
Operating Agreement

Limited Liability Corporation, or LLC, is the ideal set-up for start-up companies and small businesses because it requires the business owner to take on only limited liability for the company.

And the good news is that creating an LLC is fairly simple and inexpensive. Take note that the operations of an LLC are governed by the LLC operating agreement.

You'll therefore need to learn how to write your LLC operating agreement.

Here is a step-by-step guide:

1. Gather basic information such as the company name and location as well as the names and physical addresses of the members of your company. You should also note your agent's name.

2. Gather all financial information. This includes each member's initial contribution to the company and how much each of them will own in terms of percentage of company interest. You can choose to have either a single-member or multi-member LLC.

For example, you could choose to initially make a contribution of $100 and own a hundred percent of the company. What's important is for all company members to be included in your LLC operating agreement.

3. Choose and download a sample agreement. Of course, you can choose to write your own agreement from scratch, but working from a sample would definitely make the process much easier for you. While operating agreements aren't really that complex, the language used can be very governmental, and basing your agreement on a sample will help ensure that the language is interpreted correctly.

4. Determine if you need the services of a registered agent. Take note that there's a slight difference in the LLC laws of each state. The operating agreement typically has a space that needs to be filled in for the registered agent.

   If your state's requirements allow it, you can be the one to fill in this space.

5. Check the "Business Purpose" section of your sample agreement and make sure it includes the statement that indicates your company's purpose as engaging in lawful acts or activities for which an LLC may be formed.

   You should also check the language in the "Term" section. "Indefinitely" is commonly used for the term.
   In the terms of dissolution, "by a majority" is also commonly used.

6. You should also check the language in the "Management" section.

   A majority of small home staging businesses are managed by the members as a whole, but you also have the option of getting managers for your home staging business, especially if there are active and passive members.

   Whatever you decide, make sure your agreement contains the appropriate language as to how your company will operate.

7. Personalize the sample agreement by inserting the data from the notes you

took as per Step 1 and Step 2. Be sure to include the necessary signature lines.

8. Print the agreement as well as a list of all members with their respective addresses and then staple them together.

   Let all members sign the agreement, have it photocopied, and then provide each member with a copy.
   Be sure to keep the original somewhere safe and have additional copies in your files for reference.

Take note that this step-by-step guide does not constitute legal advice.

If there's anything about forming an LLC that you don't understand, it's still best to seek the advice of an attorney.

Top Tips for Creating Agreements

In this day and age, verbal agreements sealed with a handshake will no longer suffice regardless of how strong a friendship you may have with the person you're dealing with or how much you trust each other.

Considering this, you may want to go over the following tips on how to create agreements that are beneficial to you, your clients, your vendors, and your team members.

Get it in writing

While an oral agreement is still legal in many cases, you'd do well to guard against fading memories, changing minds, and wavering loyalties.

A written agreement duly signed by all parties involved will save you from a lot of hassle and possible heartache right from the start. You don't even have to worry about potential clients taking this the wrong way because realtors are used to signing contracts day in and day out.

Requiring a signed agreement is, in fact, part of modern-day professional protocol. Never skip the written agreement part just because you're too busy, as you're sure to regret it in the end.

Keep it simple

Contrary to what you may think, you don't really need to use a whole bunch of legal terms to make your agreement legal.

In fact, it's so much better to use simple language you and the other parties are sure to understand. It would also be a good idea to number the paragraphs in the agreement to make it easy for you to refer to specific clauses at any time.

Make sure the agreement is signed by the right person for each party involved

Technically, any company representative can legally sign an agreement. However, you'd do well to make sure you've got exactly the right person to sign the agreement and that they indicate their title on it.

For example, if the agreement is for home staging services, then the person to sign the agreement is the one paying for the services.

If the realtor and homeowner are splitting the home staging costs, then have both of them sign the agreement and make sure your agreement specifies who's responsible for what.

If you're preparing an Independent Contractor agreement, then you have to make sure a duly-authorized company representative signs the agreement.

Make sure each party is identified correctly

This tip goes hand-in-hand with Tip #3. After all, you can hardly ensure the right person signs the agreement without first identifying who the right person is.

The agreement should indicate the signatories' names and their respective roles in the company they represent. Of course, you'll have to indicate the company name along with the proper business entity as well.

Be sure to include all the important details

This tip is especially important if you're preparing an Independent Contractor agreement.

Be sure to spell out the authority and responsibilities of each party involved in the agreement. And before each party signs, make sure everyone understands every detail of the agreement and agrees to it.

Be specific about payment terms

Specify how much the paying party owes you and how often payment should be made. It's also a good idea to indicate if payment should be made in cash only or if credit card payments are acceptable. Furthermore, you should indicate what the consequences are for late payments or if the agreed service isn't delivered.

Outline a procedure for terminating

Many home stagers have a 7-day cancellation policy in place for home staging agreements, which means a party can terminate the agreement anytime within seven days of signing it.

You may also want to set a penalty for cancellations made within three days of the agreed project start date.

It's important to specify these things so your clients understand that you have strict guidelines and policies to follow so you can protect your time and cover your expenses.

Outline a procedure for resolving disputes

Specify in the agreement what you and the other signatories will do in case something goes wrong. It may be wise to handle disputes through mediation or arbitration rather than going to court. Take note, though, that arbitration can actually be more expensive than going to court in many instances, so be sure to choose your dispute resolution procedure carefully.

Identify a provision in the law that governs the agreement

If you and the other parties are based in different states, then it's important for you to choose the state where arbitration, mediation, or any other legal action should take place.

Take note that state laws can vary significantly, so you should consider them very carefully

Consider confidentiality

This tip is very important and cannot be stressed enough.

As regards anything that has to do with your home staging business, you'll definitely need a non-disclosure and confidentiality agreement, which should include the consequences in case confidentiality is breached.

You'll realise the importance of this agreement when team members decide to leave and work with another company or start their own business venture.

It's a good idea to specify a period of time within which they aren't allowed to start a competing business within a particular radius of your own home staging business.

Writing a Company Brochure

A company brochure, also known as a corporate brochure, is an excellent way of introducing your home staging business to your target market.

That is, of course, if you do it right.

The very first things you need to take into consideration are the logo, font, and color you use on your brochure.

People will only learn about your home staging business if they read the brochure, and they are more likely to read a brochure if the cover has an attractive design, which is why your choice of logo, font, and color is very important.

Take note as well that people are more likely to patronize your home staging business if you're able to build a connection with them and if you're able to establish in their minds the thought that you can be trusted.

The best way to do this using a brochure is to include pertinent information such as the background and history of your company, what you have to offer, and how you intend to deliver whatever it is you're offering.

You may also include information on how your company intends to serve the community as a whole.

Furthermore, you'll need to provide an explanation of what the brochure itself is all about.

- Is it just about the organization or does it present the products and services as well?

- Is it all about the industry and what role your company plays in its development?

- Is it for a specific event where your company is a participant or is it a detailed brochure of your company?

And of course, you'll have to tell the reader at the outset what the brochure's relevance to him is. Therefore, before you even start writing your company brochure, you'll first have to think about what you want the brochure to portray and who your target audience is.

You may want to set-up a brainstorming session with your company's key personnel for this purpose.

And take note that even as your brochure contains all the necessary information as discussed above, it should remain concise and easy to read.

You should also make it easy for the reader to select which particular piece of information he wants to read.

This can be achieved through the use of headings and sub-titles.

As long as you keep these tips in mind, you should be able to create a company brochure that truly presents your home staging business in a positive light.

Leasing Space

Having enough space for your business is not one of the most critical factors in operating your new business as you will firstly be starting from home.

However as your business grows you may need extra space so I have included advice on acquiring space in this next section.
Among these things are good visibility of the location from the street, and easy access for your customers.

You'll also have to decide if you're going to build, buy, or rent your retail sales space.
There are many advantages to renting space as opposed to buying or building.

Maintenance, flexibility, and taxes are perhaps the three most important advantages.

Maintenance

If you rent retail sales space, you'll be responsible only for a bit of routine maintenance issues like the replacement of light bulbs, repairing uninsured damages caused by negligence on your part, and cleaning the premises.

The good news for you is that major maintenance issues like electrical, plumbing, air conditioning, heating, and structural problems are the responsibility of your landlord.

This means that if your roof starts to leak, it will be your landlord's responsibility to have it repaired.

Knowing that your rent already covers major maintenance issues makes it so much easier for you to budget your company's available funds.

Flexibility

Renting space helps you avoid being forced to stay at the same location even when it's no longer practical to do so.

Even if you have a lease contract for a specific period, that's still a lot better than getting locked into a commercial mortgage.

If the demographics in your area change, then it will be much easier to relocate your home staging business if you're simply leasing or renting space.

This also holds true for the time when your home staging business has grown such that you need more space.

Furthermore, you won't have to worry about selling your existing location if you have to move to a new place, which is an issue you'll have to deal with if you own the space.

Taxes

It's very easy to understand the advantages of renting space where taxes are concerned. Rental payments are considered business expenses and are therefore deductible.

On the other hand, only the interest that you pay for commercial mortgages is deductible.

You have to consider as well, the fact that commercial property often doesn't appreciate as much as residential properties, which means your property may accrue very little equity over time.

When you weight this against the 100% deductibility of commercial rent, you'll realize how advantageous it is to simply lease retail space.

Now that you understand the benefits of leasing retail sales space, you'll have to learn how to find the perfect location for your home staging business.

Remember that leasing will affect not only your company's profit, but also its ability to grow as well as the satisfaction level of your employees.

So, before you go out looking for space to rent, you'll have to know exactly what you are looking for.

Here's how to identify the perfect retail sales space for your home staging business:

1. Determine how much space your home staging business needs now and how much it may need in the future. The rule of thumb in determining space requirements is to have 175-250 sq. ft. of space for each person who will be working at the location.

2. Contact a real estate agent and seek advice in finding a suitable commercial space.

Agents typically have the inside scoop on what'd going on in the real estate market and they can advise you properly on which particular properties are ideal for your purposes. It's a good idea to contact a real estate firm that specializes in office space rentals.

3. Discuss any necessary improvements with your potential landlord.

   Take note that improvements are usually subject to serious negotiations, especially if there are lots of vacancies. You would also do well to check out the parking space. Does the rental offer a number of slots you can set aside for yourself and your employees, or would you have to compete with the public for street parking?

4. You may be able to reduce rental cost by either sharing space or looking out for incubators. You could share your reception area, rest rooms, and conference rooms with another small firm to reduce your rental costs – that is, if you're okay with having less privacy.

Incubators are small unused areas in a larger building which are usually offered for lease at much lower costs.
These are also good options for a small home staging business like yours, provided it meets with your requirements, of course.

5. You may also want to consider renting an all-inclusive suite. The rate for executive office suites is usually higher, but they usually come fully-furnished and provide you with access to meeting rooms and office equipment, thus significantly reducing your up-front costs. Many of these suites even come with a receptionist.

6. Before signing a lease contract, be sure to review it exhaustively. Check the indicated monthly payment, how long the lease is for, what maintenance and repair concerns the landlord will be responsible for, and things like annual rent increases in accordance with inflation.

You'd also do well to check if there are provisions concerning the possibility of terminating the lease early as well as provisions regarding internet connections, cable service, telephone lines, and other company needs.

Other important details for you to review include the date of occupancy, right of refusal for the adjoining space, security, and other amenities.

7. Finally, it's a good idea for you to hire a qualified real estate attorney. Make sure the attorney specializes in negotiations for leases and that he knows your area. It's a bonus if he has dealt with the same kind of home staging business in the past. This is important because lease negotiations typically cover hundreds of terms, which makes it a definite advantage to have someone who's gone through it all before on your side.

Managing Your Employees

Once your home staging business becomes successful and grows you may need to employ staff, and you'll have to deal with managing your employees, which can be a very tricky process.

If you're not careful, you just might end up babysitting rather than running a successful home staging business venture.

This is especially true if a majority of your employees are paid very low hourly rates. You're lucky if you can hire wonderful employees who don't give you any problems.

However, you'll still have to find effective ways of keeping these wonderful employees in your home staging business, and that's where good employee management comes in.

Perhaps the most important aspect of employee management is your ability to set very clear goals and communicate your company objectives very clearly to your employees.

Take note that goal-setting and communicating objectives have to be done regularly.

The more you communicate with your employees in an honest and open manner, the easier it will be for you to manage them.

It's advisable to set monthly, quarterly, and annual goals. And you have to make sure the goals you set are mutual.

This means you should not be forcing your employees to work towards your own goals.

The employees themselves have to believe in those goals and they'll have to be taught how to adjust in case circumstances that keep them from attaining those goals suddenly arise.

Furthermore, you need to realize that goals don't really mean much unless employees' compensations are largely tied up with those goals.

The compensation may be in the form of bonuses, commissions, or salary percentages. What's important is for the employees to have a good motivation for working towards the company's goals.

It's also a good idea to hold a yearly meeting with all of your employees where an annual review will be conducted.

During this review, you should commend your employees for the things they're doing right and discuss solutions for the things that didn't quite work out.

Identifying areas of improvement and finding solutions together can give employees the assurance that they really are part of the company and that they're being valued as individuals, not just as paid workers.

Finally, another very important part of employee management is getting feedback on how YOU are doing at your job.

- How are you as a manager?

- What are you doing right?

- What else can you do to become a better manager?

You have to realize that getting feedback from your employees isn't a waste of your time. Quite the contrary, in fact.

More often than not, the best ideas for improving a home staging business come from the front-liners, as they're usually the ones who know exactly what the customers want.

How to Market Your
Home Staging Business

It's been reported that half of all home staging business closures resulted from the lack of a clear marketing plan.

Therefore, it's important for you to learn how to effectively market your home staging business so it can easily rise above the competition.

This can be done with a little help from industry experts who can assist you in generating effective advertising campaigns and marketing strategies.

Marketing your new home staging business probably ranks among the most challenging aspects of putting up a business venture, not to mention that it can also be the most fun.

You should, in fact, be excited about marketing your home staging business.

- The main purpose of marketing a home staging business is to let your target customers know that you exist and that you have a lot of benefits to offer them.

And take note that the kind of message you convey to your target market is crucial when you market a new home staging business.

Even if you're selling exactly the same service as your closest competitor, you're more likely to come out on top of the competition if you're able to come up with better marketing strategies and if you can successfully create a brand for your company.

Creating a brand for your company will make your home staging business more valuable to potential customers.

Regardless of what type of business you're into branding is still important.

In fact, the more you create an attractive personality around your company brand, the more you set yourself apart from the competition, thus giving your home staging business a much better opportunity for growth. How do you know your brand is effective?

Simple.

Market it to yourself.

Imagine that you're a would-be customer taking stock of a new player in the industry.

- Does the company brand look, sound, and feel authentic?

- Is it a fun and attractive brand?

Remember that marketing your home staging business has to be fun, so don't take it too seriously.

And even while you're working hard to create a brand, you should always remain true to yourself. That is what will make your brand truly authentic. And an authentic brand is something your competition can never take away.

Using Social Media to Market Your Business

You probably already know that social media can be a very effective marketing tool for your home staging business.

However, using social media for marketing purposes can be a bit time-consuming, so you'll really have to know what you're doing; otherwise, it can be just be a huge waste of your precious time.

You may have to spend weeks or even months familiarising your social media of choice before you can actually start using it to market your home staging business.

Above all, take note that it's not the number of connections you have that matter in marketing through social media; it's the quality of these connections.

For example, it may be enjoyable to connect with realtors in other parts of the world, but that isn't likely to increase your bottom line. To achieve that purpose, you'll have to connect with realtors within your own area of operations.

In discussing how to use social media for marketing purposes, it's best to focus on the three most popular social media sites today:

- Facebook

- Twitter

- LinkedIn

These three sites have one major advantage in common and that's the fact that they're absolutely free.

All you need to do is sign-up for an account and start learning how to use them to your advantage.

Even better news is that these three social media sites have tutorials that help you understand how to move around the platform. Now, let's take a closer at each one in turn.

Facebook

This is a social networking site that allows you to join networks organised according to city, region, workplace, or school. This is how you connect to other people using the site. You may also add friends, send messages, and update your profile to let your friends know about the latest happenings in your life.

There are plenty of home staging and real estate groups you can join on Facebook. All you need to do is type in the term "real estate groups" in the search bar and then you'll get a list of all real estate groups using the site.

Check out the ones that seem most interesting and then choose which groups to join.

Once you've joined a group, you'll have access to their members and be able to add them as friends so you get to see their profiles. It's best to look for groups with members residing within your area. The site even allows you to do a profile search according to city, state, or zip code.

Twitter

This is a micro-blogging site that allows you to send and read updates, which are referred to as tweets. These updates are text-based posts with a maximum length of 140 characters, which are displayed on your profile page and then shown to other users who have subscribed to your page.

These subscribers are known as your followers. It's often a bit challenging to express what you want to say in just 140 characters, which is why Twitter definitely calls for creativity! This difficulty notwithstanding, you'll be surprised at the amount of activity going on in this site 24/7. The good news is that you don't need other people's approval to follow them, so you can quickly build a good list of followers.

Bear in mind, though, that there's a limit to how many people you can follow each day. Furthermore, there has to be a good balance the number of people you follow and your own number of followers.

The drawback is that Twitter isn't really as organised as Facebook and LinkedIn yet. You may want to check out #realtor, #real estate, and #home staging to see if you can find interesting groups to join.

And while you can search for specific individuals on Twitter, you may also want to take advantage of add-on applications like TweetDeck to make your Twitter experience so much easier.

LinkedIn

This is a business-oriented networking site used primarily by professionals. The good news for you is that there are lots of real estate professionals using this site.

The drawback, however, is that members are generally not accessing their LinkedIn accounts as often as they do their Facebook and Twitter accounts.

Just like Facebook, this site allows you to join groups and invite people from those groups to join your network. While this site is definitely not quite as exciting as the other two, it's significantly more professional and can be extremely valuable to your home staging business.

Top tip:

Now that you know what these three social media sites are all about, you may want to take note of this time-saving tip: You can link your Facebook and LinkedIn accounts to your Twitter account so that whenever you send an update, it'll automatically appear on the two other accounts as well. What's important is for you to have fun while marketing your business on social media.

Customer Testimonials

Have you ever experienced switching the TV on in the middle of the night only to find out that there's nothing to watch but infomercials? If so, then you may have noticed that regardless of what product is being sold, most of these infomercials are likely to show testimonials from people who've tried the product.

Why is this important and what does it have to do with your home staging business?

Well, this is social proof that the product being advertised really works. The premise is that if it works for someone else then it'll surely work for you, too.

Take advantage of the same premise and collect testimonials from some of your satisfied customers – both sellers and realtors – during or after you're done staging a home for them.

You may then choose the most compelling testimonials and use them in your marketing efforts. Always remember that when people talk about your home staging business in a positive light, saying how easy you were to work with, how efficient you are, and how much you've helped them save money and sell their property at a price that was more than what they expected to get for it, other people tend to stop and actually take notice.

This is how testimonials can make marketing your business a whole lot easier. You don't have to actually hard sell your business; you simply share what other people think of you and your services.

So, if you've already started operating a home staging business but haven't gotten around to using testimonials as part of your marketing strategy, then you should start planning for it right now.

Try to come up with a system of collecting testimonials from previous and present clients. You may collect testimonials in written, audio, or video format. The good news is that you don't really have to spend too much on this marketing strategy.

In collecting audio testimonials, you can simply purchase an inexpensive digital recorder and then convert it into a file you can upload onto your business website or social media accounts. For video recording, a basic digital video camera should suffice.

To maximise the effectiveness of using testimonials for marketing purposes, it's best for you to mix it up. Arrange a good combination of written, audio, and video testimonials on your website and social networking accounts. Be creative in using the testimonials while making sure that your clients' happy thoughts and positive feedback are clearly expressed to the world.

Marketing Tactics You Should Avoid

Many individuals with a natural love and talent for decorating get into the home staging business without any marketing knowledge or business training.

Although they have the best intentions, they typically end up using some marketing tactics that usually succeed only in putting them out of business without even knowing exactly what hit them.

When you decide to make a career out of home staging, you should realise that marketing needs to be a priority in your efforts to build a solid client base. The problem is that many home stagers fail to present a professional image, thus hurting their own chances at success and casting the entire home staging industry into a bad light as well.

You probably already know of the best marketing techniques to use for growing your business. But, what you may not know is that there are also some marketing tactics you need to avoid using, as they'll only succeed in ruining your business.

Guaranteeing a Sale

It's quite amazing how people often find the simplest ways to bankrupt their own business. One of the most common ways home stagers doom their business is by guaranteeing the sale of their clients' respective homes.

When the economy is tough and the real estate market slow, it's understandable for a home seller to want some sort of guarantee, especially when they invest in home staging services. It can also be easy to understand why some home stagers jump at the chance to provide that guarantee in an effort to attract new business.

However, if you hope to stay in the business for the long term, you'll have to study the rationale behind providing sales guarantees very carefully.

The main reason why guaranteeing a sale isn't a good idea is that there are several factors involved in home staging that you don't have control over. Regardless of how well you stage a home, there will still be other factors that help determine whether it sells or not, such as the following:

- Seasons of the year – Spring break and Christmas are generally poor times for selling real estate.

- Correct pricing according to property size, location, and current market conditions

- Presence or absence of features buyers generally look for in the area. For example, a one-bedroom house isn't likely to sell well in a family neighbourhood regardless of how well it is staged.

- The real estate agent's marketing abilities. Let's face it: A property isn't likely to sell well unless it's marketed properly.

- The seller's ability to keep the property in showing-ready condition at all times

- The manner in which the seller and real estate agent handles sale negotiations; negotiations often break down for a number of different reasons that have nothing to do with staging.

> ➤ Natural disasters, political upheavals, or any significant economic event that may interfere with the real estate market

The only thing you can guarantee as a home stager is that the property will be shown in the best light when it's staged. Take note that you can only guarantee a sale if you decide to buy the property yourself! You'd do much better to gather statistics from past projects as regards the average length of time it takes for properties you stage to sell and how your statistics compare to other properties within the same price range and area during the same period.

What's Holding You Back?

Just like any business owner, you may get excited with the work for starters, love everything that comes with it, and then suddenly come to a sudden stop seemingly without any valid reason. What just happened?

The most probable explanation is that you got sabotaged by your own thinking. Yes, it's quite common.

Your own thought processes can sabotage your home staging business just when things all seem on the up and up. When you continuously play those "what if" scenarios in your head, there will come a time when you forget everything you've accomplished so far and actually feel unable to move forward with the business.

To illustrate, here are some of the most common "what if" scenarios people play in their heads all the time, particularly people in the home staging or design business:

> What if my first client arrives before I'm able to get my website up?

> What if I spend a huge amount of money on training only to find out I'm not much good at the work?

> What if my trade show booth doesn't turn up any good leads?

> What if I fail to get help on a home staging project?

➤ What if I don't win any bids for even a single home staging project during my first month of operations?

➤ What if my first client doesn't like my work?

Rather than dwelling on these negative "what if" scenarios, you should focus more on these:

✓ What if you succeed in getting your first client before your website is up? In that case, you'll do an excellent job for him and then ask for a testimonial that you can post on your website when it's finally established! You should also take this opportunity to take great before-and-after photos that you can use for building your portfolio.

✓ Remind yourself regularly that any training or short course you take for your business is an excellent investment because it enhances your natural talent and helps confirm that you are, in fact, a wonderful home stager. Think of the training program as a way for you to gain more confidence in your work and earn credentials that will help attract more clients to your business.

✓ Make sure your trade show attendees are properly screened so you can be confident of getting a number of ideal clients.

✓ When you attend a training course, make other course participants aware of your possible need for help and establish connections with them so you can call on them when the need for help does arrive. It may be a good idea to get help from a few different people to see who fits your requirements best. You could end up finding a great partner in your home staging business!

✓ Find out which home staging business currently wins the most number of bids and then find out why. The information you gather will let you know how you can set your business apart and help you find ways of winning the next bid.

✓ Is there really a reason for your client not to like your work when you're doing something you love and you've taken all the necessary steps to make sure you're the best at what you do? Most probably not.

Take a close look at what you've accomplished in your past jobs because the way you did things is most probably the way you normally do things. Focus on enhancing your strengths and then work on the things which you feel you need to improve on. Most importantly, always tell yourself you're capable of achieving your goals and making your home staging dreams come true.

You can do it...

You just have to have the confidence to start and follow a few simple rules.

Treat each customer like a VIP, provide valuable advice and offer exceptional customer service.

These should allow you to make full use of the many things that truly make a home staging business unique.

Here's a quick recap:

If you've decided for sure that home staging is the perfect business venture for you, then you may as well start learning as much as you can about the entire process of setting it up.

The good news is that setting up this kind of business may be a lot easier than you think. Staging experts are usually willing to help out newcomers like you, especially if you seek advice from those who are working in areas other than yours.

With housing prices currently falling, more and more people are seeking help in an effort to sell their homes for the best possible price. This is definitely the right time for you to enter the home staging scene.

1. Naturally, the first thing you need to do is build on what you already know about home design.

   Find experienced stagers who are willing to share their knowledge with you and teach you the ins and outs of the business.

   As much as possible, try to talk to stagers in a few different towns so you'll get a general idea of what works in a particular neighbourhood and what doesn't.

   It's also a good idea to avoid talking to someone working in the same area you plan to cover; remember that you're about to become a competitor. Take your area's housing market into consideration and learn from the mistakes of the other stagers you speak with.

2. The next step is to keep track of the latest trends in your locality's real estate market as well as those in your neighbouring towns.

It's also a good idea to discuss your ideas for the business with someone who's familiar with your area and the real estate industry. Start building a strong network with realtors in the area because they generally know what's hot and what's not in the industry. They can also be your best long-term source of home staging projects. Visit the realtors' open houses, take them to lunch, and get a feel for what they think will sell.

3. Create a business plan that will serve as your guide and keep you focused even when you have to go through tough times as you start growing your home staging business.
   Determine how much you'll need for start-up costs and then discuss how you intend to spend your capital. Determine how you'll have to spend in marketing your business to home sellers, real estate agents, and small builders. Aside from guiding you through the process of growing your business, you can also use your business plan to find investors if you feel the need for it.

4. Choose a name for your home staging business and then find out what permits and licenses you need to obtain as well as what taxes you need to pay in order to set up your business.

   It's important to make sure your business is legal to start with because launching any business without securing all the necessary legal documents beforehand can lead to some serious problems later on and may even cause the business to close down.

5. Start marketing your business.

   Get business cards made and then start distributing them to potential clients as well as other people who may be able to pass them on to your target clients.

   Create brochures as well and then hand them out along with your business cards to other businesses that may be able to help you get clients, e.g. realtors, residential contractors, painting companies, townhouse and condominium office managers, and moving companies.

When any of these businesses sends you a referral, be sure to send a thank you note. Once you start getting projects, market your business even further by creating a website and then posting before and after photos of the homes you've worked on.

Advertise your home staging venture by distributing flyers containing the name of the home staging, its location (if you have an office), hours of operation, and your business contact information.

Create publicity and attract customers by holding a mini home-makeover show at the local mall or at a nearby venue. You may also distribute flyers and business cards at the show.

6. Start collecting props to use for home staging. You'll need just about everything from pillows to furniture.

Thrift stores and moving sales usually turn up some great furniture and accessories you can buy at very low prices. Make sure the items you get are free of any stains and unpleasant odours. After all, you wouldn't want to defeat the entire purpose of staging by using smelly or dirty items.

Considering the need for props, you'll probably have to designate one room in your house for storage purposes. If there isn't any available space in your home, then you may want to consider renting storage facility or perhaps building a storage shed in your backyard. As your business grows, you may need to rent a warehouse.

7. Set your rates and make sure they cover your business costs, expenses, and payment for your efforts. Do your homework and find out what other home stagers are charging, and then make sure your rates are competitive.

Remember that setting rates too high may drive potential clients away, while setting them too low might give them the wrong impression that your work isn't really that good. You need to learn how to place the right value on your work.

8. Decide if you need an extra pair of hands to help you in staging a client's home. If so, then you may want to begin your search for an assistant by checking to see if any of your family members or friends wants an extra source of income on the side. Assisting you on a home staging job may be the perfect project for retired acquaintances and soccer moms. Home staging also often involves paint and cosmetic work, so it's also a good idea to establish a partnership with a local contractor or a local painter.

9. Conduct all the necessary research on your target market, on the competition, and on the overall demand for your products in your area before you spend any money on your business venture. Among other things, you need to make sure that the location and operational procedures you've chosen are truly what's

best for you and your business. Don't just make decisions based on general business rules or on what works for your competitors. Remember that no single strategy will ever work well for everyone, which makes it all the more important for you to find your own best practices.

10. Follow your business plan, but be sure to leave room for adjustments, considering that your market and the overall economic climate can change at any time.

11. Remember that among the most important things you need to ensure when running this type of business is that of remaining competitive.

12. Take out business insurance to cover general liability, product, property, auto, and workers' compensation (when you employ staff). This will help protect you in case of lawsuits and settlements.

Better safe than sorry.

Balanced business

Finally, you'll need to learn how to balance your business life with your home life. This is where most people encounter problems.

For example, how are you going to deal with an out-of-hours call when you're also having a few people over for dinner?

At one point or another, you're going to have to give up some things. It's a good idea to set up a schedule beforehand and let your customers know about this schedule so they're aware of the times when you won't be available.

The above information isn't meant to discourage you from pursuing your dream of running a home staging business.

It's simply meant to set the right expectations and prepare you for what might go wrong.

Knowing the things that can possibly go wrong puts you in a better position to take the necessary precautions.

Have fun being your own boss

The great thing about running a home staging business is that you get to be your own boss, create your own interior designs and earn a good income by doing something you naturally enjoy.

Running the business from home will also save you from having to rent an expensive storefront or purchase a commercial building. Of course, that's something you may want to consider as your business grows in the future.

Quality family time

A home business also has the added advantage of providing the perfect venue for you to spend some quality time with your family, as you can bond by helping each other prepare or package your business brochures and advertising paperwork.

In conclusion

When your home staging business is finally up and running, don't be afraid to always try something new.

Gather customer feedback and listen to what they have to say.

After all is said and done, you'll surely realise that running your own home staging business can be a truly rewarding experience.

It necessarily involves a lot of hard work, of course, just like any business does. In the end, though, the benefits and advantages you experience will surely be worth it.

All in all, running a home staging business may be an excellent way for you to earn a good profit while selling your customers homes fast and for a profit.

Good luck!

Made in the USA
Lexington, KY
01 September 2014